Learn how to do Automatic Writing.

A step by step course to help you access higher realms of the mind, body and spirit.

Irene Richardson

Crystal Forests

P.O. Box 1680

Frederick, MD 21702

http://www.crystalforests.com

©2007 Irene Richardson

Other books by Irene:

F.A.I.T.H. for You –

Fatherly Advice in the Heavens for You –

Inspirational Messages of Love and Guidance

ISBN0615215092

EAN-139780615215099

Acknowledgements:

First I want to thank the Big Man, my Spirit Guide Ophelia, my other Guides and Guardian Angels for their guidance and support while working on this project. They have all made me a better person.

I'd like to thank my husband Jerry and my children – Jeri, Kelly and Danny. There were many times they had gone without me while I was out helping other people. Thanks so much for being there for me and for loving me no matter what. I love you all so very much!

Finally I want to acknowledge my Mother. I know you did your best while you were able. I'm sorry I didn't have more time to spend with you. I hope you are happy where you are now. I miss you every day. I will see you when it's time to go home. In the mean time call me when you're not busy. I love you always and forever.

Note to the Reader:

The contents of this book are based on my own experiences with Automatic Writing. I am teaching you the way that I became successful with this medium.

Through dedication and discipline you too will be able to communicate with a Guide/Teacher/Person. Not everyone is successful right away, but with patience you will eventually succeed.

Good Luck as you begin to learn Automatic Writing.

For

Jeri   Kelly   Danny

Contents

Page

What is Automatic Writing?

Automatic writing is writing that is done through your hands using a pen, pencil or typing your words on a keyboard. It is words communicated to you through your mind via thought. It is called by some "trance" writing because it can be done quickly and without thought, whatever pops into your mind. Whether these messages come from the "spirit world" or the subconscious is unknown. Some people who have attempted this form of mediumship have written lengthy messages, songs, poetry, paintings and even complete novels.

It is believed that one can access their "higher self" being uninhibited by the conscious mind where you can access deep and mystical thoughts. It can also be used to access repressed memories or knowledge.

People who are familiar with automatic writing have claimed that they can access other intelligence's and entities for information and guidance. To access information that is not obtainable through the conscious mind. It is also used to develop psychic abilities.

Some skeptics consider automatic writing to be nothing more than nonsense coming from the writers mind to the writer's pen. However, to the serious student it is an invaluable tool. Thousands of people at one time or another has tried their hand at automatic writing. Whether it is through an Ouija Board, pen or computer real answers to your questions can be obtained through this type of medium.

The guides that you can draw to yourself can come from any walk of life. They can be from other worlds or other solar systems. They may have lived on the Earth in a previous lifetime. They may have never incarnated ever before. It is strictly up to you the type of Guide you can draw to yourself.

Sometimes the information you will receive will be in a language that you do not understand. Entities have also been known to communicate through drawings. You will not recognize the writing while you are doing it as it is the writing of the spirit/entity that you are allowing to communicate through you.

Some of you will feel more comfortable writing with pen and paper where others of you will feel better writing via your computer. Those of you who choose to do your automatic writing on the computer have an advantage as you will be able to save the work you do on a disc. Make sure you get in the habit of printing out your writings once they are written. Spirit has been known to erase writings. Why this happens no one knows.

Those of you who are able to evaluate your own work will know if you are dealing with a reliable source. Trying to decide who you want to contact will be your biggest question. Secondly trying to figure out what you want to learn from this being/entity will be your second biggest question. Whether it is answers to personal situations, finding out about long lost history, learning about what beings exist outside of the realm of Earth. The questions and the possibilities are endless. You are the creator of your experience.

Meditation is the key to success in Automatic Writing!

Meditation is the ability to focus our attention on only one thing. Meditation enables us to calm the mind and relax from a busy day of endless thoughts racing through our minds. It helps to make us calmer, more relaxed and relieves tension. It can help us to discover many levels of knowledge as we gain the confidence and endurance in meditating each day.

Observing the breath is a simple yet powerful type of meditation. I personally have stayed with the Breath Meditation prior to any mediumship work. I find that it helps my mind and my focus in getting into that mindset quicker.

Try to set a regular time aside once or twice each day. This is going to be your personal time for growth. Pick a time where you will not be interrupted or feel rushed to move on to something else. View this as a special and important time of day for you and you alone. Be certain that you will not be disturbed during this important time of day. Turn off the phone and try to avoid all distractions. Before you begin, try to wear loose fitting clothing. Constricting clothing can be very uncomfortable and will distract you. Find a quiet spot and sit comfortably. If you can, find a chair with a straight back. If you do not have a straight backed chair you can also achieve this by sitting cross-legged on the floor up against a wall or up against the side of a sofa. Use cushions for support if you feel you need them. When you are properly supported, you spend less time thinking about being uncomfortable and have less distracting thoughts.

Make yourself comfortable. Create a space of solitude. Light candles if you like, play soothing music. This is your time of day to do something just for you. Proceed to sit down in your comfortable spot and begin by taking a few deep breaths. Inhaling slowly and deeply through your nose and exhaling slowly through your mouth.

Now, close your eyes and begin to become aware of your breathing. Listen to the inhale and exhale of your breath. Continue to take long slow deep breaths in through your nose and out through your mouth. Let any thoughts from the day pass right through and fall to the way side. Do not dwell on anything. Try to allow yourself to "just be".

As you become aware of the gentle rise and fall of your abdomen begin taking a longer breath and begin counting slowly to yourself for a count of four as you inhale through your nose.

Hold this breath for another count of four then slowly exhale through the mouth for another count of four.

Establish a rhythm that is comfortable for you and easy to maintain. By slowly breathing in and out, you are allowing your lungs to get in harmony with your mind and body as you are doing your meditation. It also helps oxygen to go deeper throughout your body, allowing you to relax easier.

Never ever hold your breath without air in your lungs. As you are slowly exhaling you are preparing yourself for new air coming in. It is the cycle of breathing that is important - slowing breathing in counting one, two, three and four, holding the breath for a count of four and then exhaling for a count of four. Repeat this count for five to ten minutes all the while breathing and keeping your attention focused on your breath.

Start with five minute intervals until you are able to do this without any distracting thoughts to interrupt your meditation. At any point during the meditation should you find your thoughts beginning to wander, simply focus back on your breathing by counting silently to yourself a count of four. All the while inhaling and exhaling.

The goal here is to be without thought while you are doing this meditation. You are training your body and your mind to become a clear vessel for Spirit to work through and with you.

You will find that you will have good and bad days while learning to meditate. Do not become so frustrated that you quit. This is not a race. The only person you are competing with is you. These foundations are being laid for your success in contacting your Spirit/Guide or Teacher, as you practice, and progress through your meditation it will become easier and feel more natural.

Keeping track of your progress is optional. I have created a table you can use to keep track of your meditations for the first month of practice. Please go to page 56 to log your meditation practice.

Assignment One

You're first assignment will be:

Think about why you want to learn Automatic Writing. Who it is that you think you'd like to contact? What do you hope to achieve by learning Automatic Writing? Take a few days to a week to really think about this question. You will find that more questions will come to you during the week as you mull it over. Be sure to write them down.

_____

_____

_____

_____

_____

_____

_____

_____

_____

What do I hope to accomplish with Automatic Writing?

The wants and needs of individuals many times go unanswered. Unless you know how to ask for what you want! What do you hope to accomplish by using Automatic Writing?

Do you hope to become Spiritually Advanced? If that's the case- who will you contact? What questions would you ask? Is there a specific person you had in mind? Jesus? The Virgin Mary? Gandhi? Archangel Michael? Once you know who and why you can concentrate on moving further ahead.

Do you hope to contact a loved one that has passed away? People long to make contact with a loved one that has passed away wishing that they could clearly speak to them just one more time. Wishing, longing, waiting... In this situation, which loved one would you like to contact? What would you like to find out? Where they are? If they're watching over you? Who are they with? What happens after you die?

Do you hope to make contact with a Great Person that has lived on earth before that can help you with studies in another area of your life? Do you want to learn how to channel energies through yourself? Contact Mozart for Inspiration, Van Gogh if you're an artist, Abraham Lincoln?

Do you wish to make contact with beings not from our planet? Find out if there's life on Jupiter? Mars? Pluto?

As I've said before this area is a vast ocean and the possibilities are endless! I want you to take into serious consideration the type of being/entity/person that you would like to make contact with. Why do you want to make contact with this being/entity/person? What do you hope to accomplish or learn by contacting this being/entity/person? We can manifest any thing just by asking for what we want.

Please move on to Assignment Two.

Assignment Two

Now that you've given some thought as to what you'd like to accomplish in Automatic Writing. Please write down who you'd like to contact. Why you'd like to contact them, and what you would like to learn from them. It can be anywhere from a paragraph to as long as you'd like. Again careful thought should be put into this as this will decide your success in achieving the Art of Automatic Writing. Please be very specific on what you want in your guide, what you would like to learn from your guide, what previous experience this guide may have had to assist you in what you want to learn and know.

Who would you like to contact?

_____

_____

_____

_____

_____

_____

_____

Why do you wish to contact them?

_____

_____

_____

_____

_____

_____

What do you hope to achieve by making contact?

_____

_____

_____

_____

_____

_____

What qualities would you like in your contact?

_____

_____

_____

_____

_____

_____

_____

What do you want to learn from this contact?

_____

_____

_____

_____

_____

How do I go about making contact with my Guide/Teacher/Loved One?

Sometimes when I write up lessons I end up channeling information. This can happen to you too eventually. As I started planning this lesson, Spirit has chimed in and wants to speak to the students. I work with a Group of Beings Called The Council of Light. I will let them speak to you now.

Blessings to One and All-

We come here to inform you that what you are about to learn is very informative and important. The Art of Automatic Writing has been done for centuries and we have had a hand in it all of this time. When you wish to communicate with us.....
Please be sure of your intention. We are not here to amuse you, nor are we here to influence your beliefs. This is a journey that you have chosen to partake in. The call has been heard. How you go about contacting us will depend on your pureness of heart and spirit.

If you wish to find out information to hurt someone else you will not succeed. If you wish to find out secrets about someone else? You will not succeed. If you wish to learn more than you already know? You "will" succeed. Do you wish to find out about yourself? You "will" succeed. There are many ways to communicate with us. You are opening the line of communication from yourself to the unknown. Be certain that if your pursuit is to learn. You will learn! We will go about making contact with you first and foremost in your thoughts. You set the timing; you set the speed at which we will start communication. It's all up to you!! Congratulations on your choice and we look forward to working with all of you in the future. May the brightest stars shine on every single one of you as we pursue this journey together.

The Council of Light

Your Third Assignment

Not that you know how imperative it is for you to understand why you want to learn Automatic Writing. In this assignment I want you to Finally........ Write down who it is you wish to contact, why you want to contact them, what you hope to learn from the Guide/Teacher/Person that you've chosen. The actual qualities that you want in your guide/contact. Please be very specific. This can be as long or as short as you wish to write.

We will proceed in the next lesson on everything and anything that you can request from your guide/teacher/being.

_____

_____

_____

_____

_____

_____

_____

What do I ask for from my guide/teacher/person?

Here is the fun part of manifesting what you want in your relationship with your Guide/Teacher/Person. Many things have to be taken into consideration when you've decided whom you want to contact.

Has my contact lived on earth before?
Was my contact a famous person?
Did my contact do anything to change/help humanity?

In this part of Automatic Writing you get to decide who/what/where/why and how you will establish your relationship with your guide/teacher/person.

You get to make sure that what you want in your guide is provided to you.
What qualities do you want in your guide? Kindness? Sense of Humor? Disciplined? Compassionate? Loving?

You get to ask for certain circumstances of your guide such as:

I wish for a guide that has lived on earth before.
I wish for a guide that has had children.
I wish for a guide that is knowledgeable about guitar.

I wish for a guide that has never lived in a human body before.

I wish for a guide that can teach me more about myself than I do now.

You get to ask for a guide that will teach you exactly what you would like to learn about.

I wish for a guide that is knowledgeable about the world.
I wish for a guide that knows about the solar system.
I wish for a guide that can teach me about the Bible.

Pretty much you can ask for whatever you want from your guide. Please be sure it's exactly what you want. For what you ask for you will surely receive and you will have no one to blame but yourself. Think about everything and anything that you want for and from your guide, what you want to learn from your guide. Tell your guide what you hope to accomplish with them. Please move on to Assignment 4.

Assignment Four

In this assignment you should already know who or what type of Guide/Teacher/Person that you want to contact. Here you will state your requests from your guide/teacher/person. For every statement that you make to your contact you will begin your sentence with: I wish to make contact with (Fill in the blank) spirit guide that is/has (kind, lived on earth, lived in another galaxy). You must start every sentence/wish that way.

You are putting your intent out to your contact to let them know that you are almost ready to establish a relationship with them. Here you will list everything that you desire in your contact, everything you wish your contact to have, everything you wish your contact to be able to teach you, everything else that you can possibly think of that you want to do with your contact will go here.

_____

_____

_____

_____

_____

Now What?

Alright you've had plenty of time to think about everything so far! This is where you put all of your thoughts/wants/desires into motion. But first! You must learn about protection...

What is Protection? Protection is what will keep you safe while you are making contact with your Guide/Teacher/Person. This is a must!! You must learn how to protect yourself from negative influences, entities. That's why I despise Ouija boards being sold to children. They have no idea about such things! Yes there are good and bad spirits/guides/entities out there. To insure that you have a clean channel open, you will create a sacred space for yourself. This can be done in several ways.

1. Decide where it is in your home that you wish to do your writing. Make sure that it is a comfortable place. When I started I worked at my kitchen table. I eventually developed my skill to working on the computer.

2. I always make sure that I have a white candle with me; this helps me get focused and allows my intent to flow better. I also like to light sage and cleanse the area that I am working in.

3. Make sure there are no distracting noises. Turn off the TV, radio; take the phone off the hook.

4. Set up your work surface for writing. I like using a 5 subject note book and pen. If you wish to try the computer by all means do so. If you wish to use pencil and paper do so. This is up to you. Use what you are most comfortable with. Do you like having a sacred statue around you? Go get it!! Are there certain crystals /stones that you like near you? Go get them. Have a picture of someone that you want to contact? Use it! Create your sacred space for writing. Decorate it how you wish, surround yourself with things that you feel give you power.

5. Once you have set up your sacred space....... You will begin your Ceremony for Protection. Seat yourself comfortably, light your white candle. The prayer of protection is:
Mother/Father/God as I sit here in peace love and harmony, I ask that my (Fill in the blank) Spirit Guide/Guardian Angel/Loved One surround and protect me.

Dear God let your white light surround and protect me. (All the while visualizing white light coming from the heavens, surrounding your entire being from head to toe. Do this visualization until it is completed. Do not do this half heartedly.) Thank you for any help that I may receive during this session. Amen.

Memorize this prayer of protection. If you feel that you would like to create your own then do so.   Always protect yourself prior to any kind of psychic work.

Please proceed to your Fifth Assignment.

Your Fifth Assignment

For your fifth assignment organize your sacred space. Gather your materials that you would like to be surrounded prior to officially beginning your first Automatic Writing Session. Learn your prayer of protection by heart. Practice your Breath Meditation. Decide how you will do your automatic writing..... pen and paper? Pencil and Paper? Computer? Upon doing all of the above. There is no right or wrong way. Do what's comfortable for you!! Proceed to lesson 6 after you have finished this assignment.

Double checking your work.

By now you should know who you want to contact. All of your requests should be written out. The type of guide you want, the characteristics in the type of guide you want. The knowledge that this type of guide may have. What you would like to learn from your guide. What you want to accomplish.

Why is it so important? It is imperative that you establish exactly what you want. That you are focused in your intentions. As the power of thought is so powerful. You will find out how powerful once you get established in your Automatic Writing.

If you are not specific enough you will draw to yourself exactly what you ask for. So make sure at this point in time that everything you want to happen will!! Every single possible detail must be accounted for.

Knowing this, Take out your paper and again go over everything that you have written so far. This is your last double check to make sure that you are drawing to you exactly what it is you want to achieve.

I have my original list from back in 1989. This is something that will be part of your history. Five years from now you will be amazed at how far you have come.

If you feel that your list is finished - You are now ready to start the process. It will be 5 more days before you will actually be able to sit down and do your automatic writing. Now is the time where you will verbally state what it is you want to draw to yourself.

If you feel that your list isn't finished - go back and start from the beginning and reevaluate your work up until this point. There is no rush!! Proceed to Assignment Six.

Assignment Six

Your assignment for the next five days will be to take your list, perform your protection ceremony, sit at your sacred space and verbally state out loud everything that is on your list three times each day. This must be done every day for the five days three times a day. Do not read your list three separate times during the day. You must read aloud your list three times back to back.

I would also choose a time that will be convenient for you to work in at the same time every day. Your focus and your intention are critical right now. You are stating to the Universe that you want to make contact. You are letting them know that you are willing enough to be open minded, willing to step out of your comfort zone. You are saying to them I'm here and I want to work with you.

It's very important that you do your homework to achieve success in Automatic Writing.

Finally the real deal!

If you've made it this far in the course then I know you've done your homework! There must not be any doubt in your mind that you haven't given every possible consideration into what you want to achieve. Now is the time where you will actually sit down at your sacred space, perform your protection ceremony and make your first attempt at contacting your Guide/Teacher/Person.

Your first Automatic Writing Session should go as follows:

1. Make sure that anything that could be distracting is turned off.

2. Organize your sacred space if it isn't already organized. Some people have to work at their kitchen table. That's fine!! Just go ahead and set it up. Light your white candle.

3. Proceed to sit down with your notebook/computer at hand.

4. Those of you who are using a note book on the first page of your note book - you will dedicate your book to the Guide/Teacher/Person that you want to work with. Write them a letter of what you hope to get out of all of this. Thank them for their help. Sign and date it. Those of you who are using

your computer you too create a file specifically for your Automatic Writing. On the first page dedicate this time to your Guide/Teacher/Person. Tell them what you hope to accomplish. Thank them for their help, sign and date it.

5. At this point in time you will try and clear your mind of all distracting thoughts (This is where your practice for meditation will come in very handy. The ability to quiet your mind and request the help of your Guide/Teacher/Person will flow so much smoother.) Take this time to do your breath meditation. Clear your mind of all thoughts. Focus on your white candle. Close your eyes breathe slowly and deeply. In through your nose and out through your mouth. Do this until you feel that you're in the right state of mind to begin your Automatic Writing session.

Next, you will verbally state aloud your prayer of protection. After your prayer of protection just sit there for a moment with your eyes closed and concentrate on your Guide/Teacher/Person coming to you to begin communication with you. You have just spent the previous 5 days telling them what you want now you will find out if the work that you have done will come to fruit.

6. Open your eyes. On your paper write down your first question that you have for your Guide/Teacher/Person. Go

down to the next line and wait for your pen/pencil to start moving. Sometimes your first contact will simply be squiggles and lines. Hold your pen loosely allowing the contact to work through you. You will feel an impulse to start moving your hand. Just let it happen. If you begin to have thoughts come to your mind, write those down too. Your contact might communicate with you that way also. Those of you who wanted to work on computer - type down what thoughts come to your mind. It's a little more difficult to get going by using the computer at first so you may want to try and start with the pen and paper instead.

7. Allow yourself at least 15 minutes to get a response from your Guide/Teacher/Person. If you are finding that nothing is happening, don't get frustrated!! You are establishing a different way of communication. For some people it will happen immediately. For others it will take some time.

8. Slowly build up your time of working with your Guide/Teacher/Person. If you find that you are having success immediately? By all means spend as much time as you want. If you are not having success, immediately stop what you are doing and try again tomorrow. Not everyone will be able to do this from the start. That is normal.

I wish every single one of you success in your new venture of Automatic Writing. Love and Light to all of you.

If you wish to ask me any questions feel free to contact me at: Irene@crystalforests.com

My first and only list to my Spirit Guide.

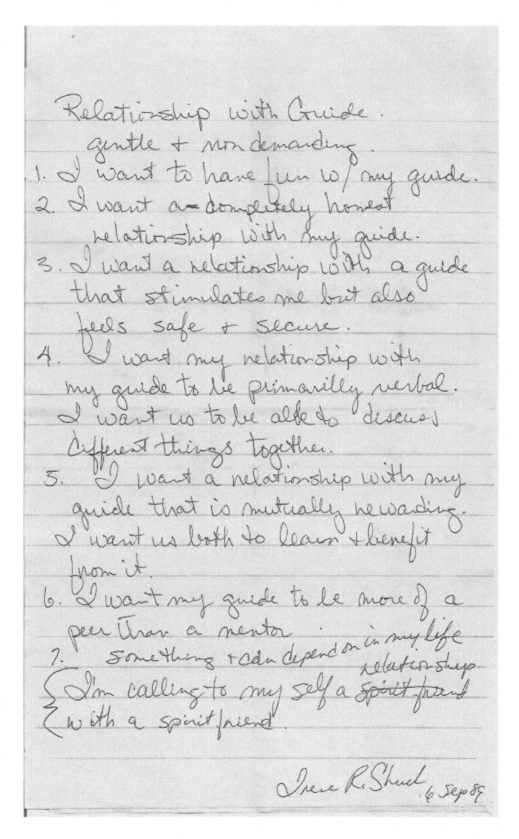

Relationship with Guide.
   gentle + non demanding.
1. I want to have fun w/ my guide.
2. I want a completely honest
   relationship with my guide.
3. I want a relationship with a guide
   that stimulates me but also
   feels safe + secure.
4. I want my relationship with
   my guide to be primarilly verbal.
   I want us to be able to discuss
   different things together.
5. I want a relationship with my
   guide that is mutually rewarding.
   I want us both to learn + benefit
   from it.
6. I want my guide to be more of a
   peer than a mentor.
7.   something I can depend on in my life
   I'm calling to my self a ~~spirit friend~~ relationship
   with a spirit friend.

               Irene R. Shuck, 6 Sep 89

What I Want To Learn —

1. I would like to develop my
   healing abilities
2. I would like to learn to have out of
   body experiences.
3. I would like to learn foreign languges
4. I would like to learn ~~to deal~~ how
   to deal with difficult people.
5. I would like to learn to play
   the flute.
6. I would like to learn to become
   very successful in my work
7. I would like to develop my
   communication skills with people
8. I'd like to learn to communicate
   with animals.

I'm calling to myself a spirit friend
who can.

Irene R. Shush 6 Sep 89

60

Qualities in a Guide.

1. I want my guide to be humorous + playful

2. I want my guide to be patient + caring.

3. I want my guide to know about medicine & healing.

4. I want my guide to be honest with me + to point out my strenghs + weaknesses

5. I want my guide to know about foreign languages.

6. I want my guide to be humble.

7. I ~~want my~~ guide to be in the ~~human chaing~~ evolution particularly ~~on earth~~ has lived on earth.

8. I want my guide to ~~be~~ be musically inclined.

9. has been a parent

10. { I am calling to myself a spirit friend who is

Irene R. Shuck
6 Sep 89

61

Meditation Practice Log

Date:
Time:
Length of Meditation:
Any distractions?
Did anything happen during your meditation?

Meditation Practice Log

Date:
Time:
Length of Meditation:
Any distractions?
Did anything happen during your meditation?

Meditation Practice Log

| Date: |
| Time: |
| Length of Meditation: |
| Any distractions? |
| |
| |
| Did anything happen during your meditation? |
| |
| |
| |
| |
| |
| |
| |
| |
| |
| |
| |
| |
| |
| |

Meditation Practice Log

Date:
Time:
Length of Meditation:
Any distractions?
Did anything happen during your meditation?

Meditation Practice Log

Date:
Time:
Length of Meditation:
Any distractions?
Did anything happen during your meditation?

Meditation Practice Log

Date:
Time:
Length of Meditation:
Any distractions?
Did anything happen during your meditation?

Meditation Practice Log

Date:
Time:
Length of Meditation:
Any distractions?
Did anything happen during your meditation?

Meditation Practice Log

Date:
Time:
Length of Meditation:
Any distractions?
Did anything happen during your meditation?

Meditation Practice Log

Date:

Time:

Length of Meditation:

Any distractions?

Did anything happen during your meditation?

Meditation Practice Log

Date:	
Time:	
Length of Meditation:	
Any distractions?	
Did anything happen during your meditation?	

Meditation Practice Log

Date:
Time:
Length of Meditation:
Any distractions?
Did anything happen during your meditation?

Meditation Practice Log

Date:
Time:
Length of Meditation:
Any distractions?
Did anything happen during your meditation?

Meditation Practice Log

Date:

Time:

Length of Meditation:

Any distractions?

Did anything happen during your meditation?

Meditation Practice Log

Date:
Time:
Length of Meditation:
Any distractions?
Did anything happen during your meditation?

Meditation Practice Log

Date:
Time:
Length of Meditation:
Any distractions?
Did anything happen during your meditation?

Meditation Practice Log

Date:
Time:
Length of Meditation:
Any distractions?
Did anything happen during your meditation?

Meditation Practice Log

Date:
Time:
Length of Meditation:
Any distractions?
Did anything happen during your meditation?

Meditation Practice Log

Date:
Time:
Length of Meditation:
Any distractions?
Did anything happen during your meditation?

Meditation Practice Log

| Date: |
| Time: |
| Length of Meditation: |
| Any distractions? |
| |
| |
| Did anything happen during your meditation? |
| |
| |
| |
| |
| |
| |
| |
| |
| |
| |
| |
| |
| |
| |

Meditation Practice Log

Date:
Time:
Length of Meditation:
Any distractions?
Did anything happen during your meditation?

Meditation Practice Log

Date:
Time:
Length of Meditation:
Any distractions?
Did anything happen during your meditation?

Meditation Practice Log

Date:
Time:
Length of Meditation:
Any distractions?
Did anything happen during your meditation?

| Date: |
| Time: |
| Length of Meditation: |
| Any distractions? |
| |
| |
| Did anything happen during your meditation? |
| |
| |
| |
| |
| |
| |
| |
| |
| |
| |
| |
| |
| |
| |

Meditation Practice Log

Date:	
Time:	
Length of Meditation:	
Any distractions?	
Did anything happen during your meditation?	

Meditation Practice Log

Date:

Time:

Length of Meditation:

Any distractions?

Did anything happen during your meditation?

Meditation Practice Log

Date:
Time:
Length of Meditation:
Any distractions?
Did anything happen during your meditation?

Meditation Practice Log

Date:
Time:
Length of Meditation:
Any distractions?
Did anything happen during your meditation?

Meditation Practice Log

Date:

Time:

Length of Meditation:

Any distractions?

Did anything happen during your meditation?

Meditation Practice Log

Date:
Time:
Length of Meditation:
Any distractions?
Did anything happen during your meditation?

Meditation Practice Log

Date:
Time:
Length of Meditation:
Any distractions?
Did anything happen during your meditation?

Meditation Practice Log

| Date: |
| Time: |
| Length of Meditation: |
| Any distractions? |
| |
| |
| Did anything happen during your meditation? |
| |
| |
| |
| |
| |
| |
| |
| |
| |
| |
| |
| |
| |

Meditation Practice Log

Date:
Time:
Length of Meditation:
Any distractions?
Did anything happen during your meditation?

Meditation Practice Log

Date:

Time:

Length of Meditation:

Any distractions?

Did anything happen during your meditation?

Meditation Practice Log

Date:

Time:

Length of Meditation:

Any distractions?

Did anything happen during your meditation?

Meditation Practice Log

Date:

Time:

Length of Meditation:

Any distractions?

Did anything happen during your meditation?

Meditation Practice Log

Date:

Time:

Length of Meditation:

Any distractions?

Did anything happen during your meditation?

Meditation Practice Log

Date:
Time:
Length of Meditation:
Any distractions?
Did anything happen during your meditation?

Meditation Practice Log

Date:
Time:
Length of Meditation:
Any distractions?
Did anything happen during your meditation?

Meditation Practice Log

Date:
Time:
Length of Meditation:
Any distractions?
Did anything happen during your meditation?

Meditation Practice Log

Date:
Time:
Length of Meditation:
Any distractions?
Did anything happen during your meditation?

Meditation Practice Log

Date:
Time:
Length of Meditation:
Any distractions?
Did anything happen during your meditation?

Meditation Practice Log

Date:
Time:
Length of Meditation:
Any distractions?
Did anything happen during your meditation?

Meditation Practice Log

Date:
Time:
Length of Meditation:
Any distractions?
Did anything happen during your meditation?

Meditation Practice Log

Date:
Time:
Length of Meditation:
Any distractions?
Did anything happen during your meditation?

Meditation Practice Log

Date:
Time:
Length of Meditation:
Any distractions?
Did anything happen during your meditation?

Meditation Practice Log

Date:
Time:
Length of Meditation:
Any distractions?
Did anything happen during your meditation?

Date:
Time:
Length of Meditation:
Any distractions?
Did anything happen during your meditation?

Meditation Practice Log

Date:

Time:

Length of Meditation:

Any distractions?

Did anything happen during your meditation?

Meditation Practice Log

Date:
Time:
Length of Meditation:
Any distractions?
Did anything happen during your meditation?

Meditation Practice Log

| Date: |
| Time: |
| Length of Meditation: |
| Any distractions? |
| |
| |
| Did anything happen during your meditation? |
| |
| |
| |
| |
| |
| |
| |
| |
| |
| |
| |
| |
| |

Meditation Practice Log

| Date: |
| Time: |
| Length of Meditation: |
| Any distractions? |
| |
| |
| Did anything happen during your meditation? |
| |
| |
| |
| |
| |
| |
| |
| |
| |
| |
| |
| |
| |
| |
| |

Date:
Time:
Length of Meditation:
Any distractions?
Did anything happen during your meditation?

Meditation Practice Log

Date:	
Time:	
Length of Meditation:	
Any distractions?	
Did anything happen during your meditation?	

Meditation Practice Log

Date:
Time:
Length of Meditation:
Any distractions?
Did anything happen during your meditation?

Date:

Time:

Length of Meditation:

Any distractions?

Did anything happen during your meditation?

Meditation Practice Log

Date:

Time:

Length of Meditation:

Any distractions?

Did anything happen during your meditation?

Here's a preview of my

next book

F.A.I.T.H.

For You

F.A.I.T.H. For You

Over the years I've come to know a lot of things in my life. I've experienced many things, and I have met many fascinating people. I've always known there's more to life than what can be seen by the human eye. There's more to life than the simple understanding of you are born, you grow, you live, you love, you laugh, you work, and ultimately you die. What get's us through all of these aspects of life?

Is it our family? Is it our friends? Is it our jobs? What keeps us all functioning day to day, week to week and year to year? What do all of our lives have in common? What is the ultimate goal for each and every one of us?   How are we shaped into what we grow into as adults? How do our lives in early childhood affect who we are as adults?   What is the divine plan in motion for each and every human being on this great planet of ours?

I've thought about many of these questions over the years. I've read many books to bring my understanding of the self, and it's relationship to the Universe. I've observed people every where I go. I love watching people. I love studying the dynamics of the human condition. Still we all have a common thread that lives within each and every one of us. We all want to be loved, we all want recognition, we all want prosperity and we are all afraid to reveal to another person who we truly are.

Who can we be honest with? Who can we turn to in our darkest hour? Who can we tell our deepest darkest secrets to? Who is it that we trust with our soul? Our whole being? Who loves us no matter what? What drives us? If you are honest with yourself you are probably answering each of these questions with one or two answers.

1. No one
2. God or your higher power

The title of this book is called F.A. I. T. H. for You. Have you ever asked yourself what that word means? To have it or not. To know someone that has it or not. Faith in what? Faith in yourself? Faith in your family, your job, your friends or faith in yourself. Faith is something that is inside you. If you've lived a life of being told you were no good, if you've lived your life being told anything that is negative who do you lean on? Who do you go to for reassurance? Do you consider yourself religious or spiritual? Have you ever felt you were not good enough to even consider talking to your Higher Power? Good enough not only to ask the questions but to get an answer back?

What if you could get an answer back? What if everything you've ever had a question to you could simply ask and hear the answer? Perhaps you can hear the answer. Do you trust what you hear? Do you have enough Faith inside you to trust that you are actually hearing from your higher power? If you do – do you actually listen to what is said to you and follow through? Let's discuss F.A.I.T.H. a little further.

Fatherly Advice In The Heavens is for you, if you are feeling these things inside of you.

My entire life I have searched for meaning.   Seeking that connection to a higher power that guides me effortlessly, compassionately and with an unconditional love that no matter what I am thinking, no matter what I am doing at the end of the day I know "Someone has my back".

Fatherly Advice in the Heavens are simple words of advice from my higher power that I am choosing to share with the world. I invite you to contemplate this simple advice.

May you find your path to greatness…

Made in the USA
Monee, IL
07 May 2022